Inspire your way through

The Storm. . .

Copyright © 2018 by Tomika Y. Reid

ISBN-13: 978-0-9975290-2-9

Library of Congress Control Number: 2020900123

Published by Tomika Reid

Printed in the United States of America 2020- First Edition

Front Cover Design: Tomika Reid and Ronald Comeau

Back Cover Design: Tomika Reid

Dedication

In honor of my mom, with eternal love.

Introduction

Inspire your way through The Storm is a quote and poem guide, written by Tomika Reid.

Tomika found her way through the storms she faced by inspiring herself, wanting to help others, holding on to her faith in God, being strong for her daughters and still wanting to make her mom proud.

Tomika decided to inspire others the day she found out she can write her own quotes; she noticed her quotes was helping others. What a way to make the world a better place, she thought.

In 2014, Tomika sat on the bench in the park across the street from where she lived, as she watched her daughters play, she thought of her mom and how many times she listened to her say, "It's going to be okay" when her first daughter father passed away, or "I'm so proud of you" when she and her first daughter father got their own apartment together, things were going great for them three as a family, and Tomika's mom saw it.

Her mom would always say such powerful words to her, they were powerful because it made her feel good, Tomika thought of those words, envisioned her mom saying them to her with a smile that day, but then she questioned, "How could my mom be proud of me now

that everything has fallen apart?" ... "I don't have a job, I don't have any money, I don't have a vehicle anymore, my children fathers are deceased, I could possibly lose my apartment." Tomika thoughts were going through her mind uncontrollably.

Although, her mom wasn't there in the flesh, she accepted the fact that the way her mom felt about her when she was alive, still mattered.

Tomika sat reminiscing over the good moments she and her mom shared, wishing her mom was there, so she could ask what she should do. During this season in her life, the storms were raging, and she needed it to pass through.

Tomika thought, "I know my mom is still proud of me because I am not giving up."

Tomika continued sitting on the bench watching her daughters play, thinking about her mom. Suddenly, she took her phone and typed some words in. She read it to herself and it made her smile. "If it can make me smile, why not use it to make someone else smile," she thought.

Tomika took her words of inspiration to social media. She wasn't sure if anyone would like it, but she posted anyway. A couple of minutes after posting, she received twenty likes. A person commented "I needed this." Afterwards, Tomika's cousin stated, "I didn't know my cousin was quotable." After seeing that, Tomika wrote her initials with every quote she posted going forward. She dedicated herself to write more quotes daily to inspire, not only herself, but others who were silently going through their own storm(s).

She owned up to her cousin's words and became a woman with quotes of her own. She enjoyed inspiring and helping others move forward in life knowing no matter what, NEVER GIVE UP.

Tomika has also written poems people enjoyed reading. She remembered a person telling her, "You are the next Maya Angelou (may she rest in peace)."

Tomika loved Maya Angelou, still does. She always wished to meet her before she passed away. Maya Angelou's life still lives on through the people who loves her dearly. Tomika is inspired by the late Maya Angelou, and she will continue inspiring others through her words of inspiration to keep them INSPIRED, MOTIVATED, ENCOURAGED and UPLIFTED.

To ALL my readers,

Thank you for taking the time to open this book to inspire your way through your storm(s).

The quotes and poems in this book have inspired me to keep pushing, to never give up and to know that it will get better because "after the storm becomes a beautiful rainbow." I believe it does get better. You tend to grow through what you go through, face the lessons that are to be learned, and cope with the loss of a loved one, because you know your loved one wouldn't want you to be sad. I believe everything happens for a reason. Life happens, and if it's beyond your reach, let it go or turn it into something positive.

Remember to forgive, for YOU so you can move on and be the best you can be.

I hope you will be inspired to never give up and enjoy this read. Always hold on to your faith and believe that no matter what, if you keep going it will get better. I am a living testimony. I am Still Standing, and you can too. You got this!

Peace, Light, Blessings and Much Love,

Tomika Reid

"When the world feels like it's on your shoulder don't stress, brush it off, give it to God and keep moving"

I am missing you on this beautiful day

I wish you never had to go away

I know you will always be in my heart

for that your love is here to stay

I couldn't help but put this shirt on today

I love you Mom, always forever and a day.

Cherish every moment

you have with your mom

because when she's gone. . .

All you have left is the memories.

"Strength comes from never giving up no matter the circumstance"

She keeps her head

held high

smile on her face

leaving no trace of

hurtful and painful

places two feet on

the move because

she knows she's

destined for

greatness nothing

and no one can

stop this girl she is

unstoppable

"You can brighten

someone's day

with a simple

smile"

Remove your frown

turn it upside down

smile

God is blessing you

right now

"You may be

broken down only

to be built back up

stronger and wiser

than ever before"

We live

We learn

We grow

We fall

We get back up

stand tall amongst it all

We laugh

We smile

We cry

We let go

We love we hurt

We gain strength through it

all

"It's not about what

you go through in life

it's how you

handle it"

*Life may take you through twist
and turns*

ups and downs

*you may even get thrown against
some curveballs*

but you must stay strong

*hold on stand tall through your
storm*

*If God lead you to it, you have the
power to get through it*

"Clear your mind

keep your head

held high towards

the sky, think

positive dream big

and do know

there is no limit to

what you can do"

When your mind is clear

your vision is clear

when your vision is clear

you think possibilities

when you think possibilities

you dream big

when you dream big

you smile

you realize there is no limit to what you can do

know anything is possible

"What you want in life

speak it into existence

speak positive

energy into the universe

and hold on to your faith-
Believe"

Focus on your purpose

dreams and aspirations

anything else is a

no-win situation

"Trust the process

you are blessed

sometimes you

must dig deep

within to find that

you do have

strength and

courage to keep going"

Push for whatever

you want in life as

hard as you can try

your best at

whatever you do

never give up

because of the

process soon you

will see some

progress

"One step

just one step

you can do it

God will help you

along the way"

A rough road can

lead to an amazing

destination stay in

total concentration

be patient, focus

and be dedicated

"Give more

expect less

or nothing at all

never expect more or the same as you would do or give;

Expectations leads to Disappointments;

free your mind from hatred and free your mind from worries

everyone doesn't have a good heart as you"

What you give away you will get back

What you sow you will reap

What you do for others

God will do for you

"Never let

opinions of others

define who you

are, you know who you are"

Trust your heart

and soul allow

your imagination

to soar never let

anyone stop you

from imagining the

unimaginable

"One day you will

find that there is

purpose in the pain

you had to

endure"

When you wake

up in the morning

and feel your heart

beating know that

there is purpose

there is hope there

is love you can do

you can forgive

you can let go you

can move on you can trust and

believe God knows your heart,

and everything will be okay

"Yesterday was yesterday

past and memory

tomorrow is tomorrow, not

promised today is today

enjoy every moment"

Each new day brings a new

start to new possibilities

never let anyone come

between you and your

abilities can't you see God

has given you another

chance dance and be

thankful for what's in your

hand enjoy every moment

before it's too late stand

and push forward go and

be great

"Prayer and action work good together don't just sit there and expect something to happen you have to go and get it"

Choices

you have

the right to

choose, sink or

swim either win or

lose

"You are the only one responsible for your happiness, do something that makes you happy"

Be content

happiness starts

within, my friend

start this day with

a smile, choose

happiness, don't

be sad, be glad in this

"You can't see up

when looking

down, keep your

head held high and your

chin up because you are

stronger than you think"

Every morning you

are blessed to see

another day Pray

and thank God for

this day, look in

the mirror, know

and believe that

everything is going

to be okay say to

yourself, I love

myself I am too

blessed to be

stressed and no

matter the mess I

am strong and

courageous

enough to get

through this mess

"A champion does not fold

when faced with challenges

he or she fights"

Channel your energy towards the light of positivity

Leave the darkness of fear and doubt into the negative wind

Never let it slip in Through the soul of which your body control

Take control of what comes and goes

Your spirit, Your soul, Your body one whole

The mind, the goal, your future unfold

Your thoughts, your dreams Things are glistening

Are you listening?

Find possibilities in all things

Let it remain

Conducive to the brain

Divine thoughts are everything

Always remain positive

Keep the energy flowing

Smile glowing, knowing

That life can be a mess

*Do your best, don't stress You're blessed,
pass the test*

Become fearless

"You may not be

there yet, but

you'll get there

keep pushing"

I know you are saying to yourself

why is it taking long? You must stay

strong, keep pushing, the time will

come, yet you will see, don't get

discouraged, let the powers that be

because you have the power to

believe and achieve

"Sometimes you must

change you or try

something new in order to

change your situation"

*Do something that make you feel
good inside*

*something that make you smile
on the outside*

*something that makes you the
happiest*

unable to let go

"Never limit

yourself on what

you can do or how

far you can go

anything is

possible"

A mind is a terrible thing to waste

it is powerful

believe in yourself

achieve the impossible

"Don't focus on where you come from focus on where you are going"

If you envisioned it

dream it

if you can dream it

believe in it

if you can believe in it, birth it

if you can birth it nurture it

if you nurture it

let it grow

if you let it grow, manifest

soon you will reap

what you've sown

"The pain you had to endure can't compare to the joy that's coming"

When things go wrong

as they sometimes will

don't give up based on how you feel

"Life is a blessing

itself anything else

good that comes

out of it is a

bonus"

If you've been blessed to

see another day

that's a shout to say HOO-RAY!

*Life is a blessing and it has a lot
to offer*

*it's up to you to become the
author*

*you have the right to make
things right*

put up a fight

*challenges will come up against
you that's a part of life*

you got this

make the best of it

*don't beat yourself up trying to
resist it,*

It's life

"Fill your mind

with positive

thoughts surround

yourself with

positive people

allow your heart to

open up to all the

positive energy the

world can bring"

Take all negativity out of your life

choose what make you happy

positivity will follow

keep pushing like there's no tomorrow

"As we walk

through this

journey, we call life

we must walk by

faith and not by

sight"

A strong woman is a beautiful woman

who conquers it all

stands tall, after every fall and keep walking

like nothing ever happened

"God places goals,

visions, dreams,

talents, hobbies

and desires in us

for a reason don't

ignore it birth it"

*Always take the necessary steps
to make your dreams come true*

*even if the steps are very small,
still...*

*take them no matter what you're
just a step closer to making your
dreams come true*

never give up on you

"In the midst of troubles know that God is working on something for your own good hold on change will come"

Stay calm like the water

relax your mind

enjoy peace and love

leave the bad things behind

"No matter the pain no matter the struggle there is a perfect place fit perfectly just for you don't crumble"

Sometimes in life

you feel like you

are losing a battle

life has shaken you

up like a baby

shaking a rattle

hold on and stay

strong it won't be

too long God is

going to work it all

out you will then feel reborn

"Each new day is a new beginning make today great"

Hard times and struggles are not

the ending to your story

Joy, Peace and Happiness

are coming give God the glory

"You may come

against opposition

it may knock you

down but there is

always a way to

get back up and

rebuild"

Be strong my sister

be bold and brave

roar like a lion be

not afraid

"Embrace life with open arms and acceptance of what's to come"

*Open your eyes, visualize, realize
you can make it happen*

*get to clapping only you can
make things happen*

*be proud of what you can do
accomplish and make your
dreams come true*

*don't demolish the vision polish
the vision*

*let the world know who hand is in
it*

*oversee the vision make the right
decisions*

embrace the good in you

*creative people always seemed to
be misunderstood*

but it's all good

*because we have the power to
create*

don't hate

*we all can create it's never too
late*

"Never let discouragement take away your joy and energy to fulfilling your dreams"

Feel confident

making your

dreams come true

you don't need no one else's
approval

do you and pursue

whatever it is

you want to do

it won't be easy

but I am telling you

just believe in you

"There are choices in life in which you can control but if it's beyond your reach learn to let it go"

For every sunset,
There is a sunrise,
For every downfall
There is an uprise
For every setback
There is a comeback
For every tear drop
There is a smile
There is a smile
Waiting to appear on your
beautiful faces
Leaving no trace of hurtful and
painful places,
It amazes me what you gain after
all of the pain,
Strength, Courage, and Wisdom
with no one else to blame, We
grow through what we go
through and nothing remains the
same,
change after change, after
change, after change, people,
places and things, nothing
remains the same Change the
game and never give up, God got
you so toughen up, You can do
this, believe in yourself, God
makes no mistakes so open up be
a blessing, live and learn life

lessons, no stressing, and every day you wake up, say God, thank you for this beautiful blessing

"No matter what

age you are you

can achieve your

dreams it's never

too late"

*Feel confident in your dreams and
aspirations let go of any doubt
you might be facing there's
nothing wrong with chasing your
dreams by any means do what
you need in order to succeed*

"You must give God something to bless and in order to do that sometimes you must take a leap of faith"

Hold on to your faith

it will give you hope to believe

that everything will be okay

"Never expect someone to understand your journey unless they walked a mile in your shoes"

Walk a mile in my shoes

don't be no fool

*and assume you know what I
been through*

once you know

you'll understand

why I move the way I do

you must go through it

to understand

*see what I see through my eyes
feel what I feel through my cries*

then, you'll know why

*I am the way I am and how I feel
on the inside*

"Sometimes you must pat yourself on the back, encourage yourself, be proud of yourself speak victory over yourself"

Yes, you,

you are unstoppable

and capable

of doing anything

you put your mind to

believe in you

"Waking up this morning is

a blessing, confirmation,

knowing that no matter

what life throws at you

today, you must keep

going"

Blessings to see another

day confirmation knowing

that everything is going to

be okay God is not through

with you, you are here for a

reason, this may not be

your season, but please

keep believing, purpose is

the key, believe in the

power of your dream, it

won't be easy please

believe me but you are

stronger than you think

"Take pride in

your own abilities.

You can do and

become anything"

Keep the fire

burning for

whatever sparks

your soul, allow

your heart desires

to flame as your

future unfold

"Never stress over

something beyond your

reach; Woosah, take a deep

breath. Breathe, believe

and have faith. Know that

God makes no mistakes"

God already know the path of your journey

and your destination

trust and believe that your current situation

isn't all of what it may seem

God is on your team

Trust your journey

Trust your creator

Trust the process don't stress

"You never know

where life will take

you but whatever

you do, you must

keep going"

Life is a journey you must make it through, either crawling or walking you must take the step

take a single step you never know what's next, you might come across something you never thought you would, you might ease the pain you never thought you could

keep going and enjoy the journey

growing and learning twisting and turning it's all a part of the process,

don't stress, it may take some time for you to see some progress, no

matter what you do, be true and always do your best in whatever you do

"When you're focused on the mission there's no time for competition"

Visions and Dreams

Visions and Dreams

never be afraid to follow your dreams

be open to your visions

follow your dreams

turn it all into reality

"Patience is a very tough lesson but it's all good because after the wait becomes a beautiful blessing"

Be open to the blessings

live and learn life lessons

no stressing

*be open and willing to making
your dreams come true*

as the writer of this book

I am here to tell you

*I believe in you please know that
patience is a virtue*

"Sometimes you just have to smile through it all"

Wake up with a smile

a joyful heart

*allow the positive energy to hit
you like a good morning cool
breeze*

so-refreshing

"Don't throw the towel in keep fighting until victory is won"

*God's power is made perfect
when you're weak*

*it's during those darkest
movements*

toughest times

*you'll find that God is the only
way*

a powerful force

that'll take you from rock bottom

to the top of the mountain

"When you pray it's a peaceful moment of tranquility and serenity"

*Prayer and meditation is the key
to welcoming*

peace, serenity and tranquility

into your mind

*take some time away from the
noise of the world*

to receive that inner peace

*release anything that doesn't
serve you any good*

"In life you'll find that the pieces to the puzzle are scattered everywhere but if you keep going and never give up, you'll also find that those same pieces will come together as one"

*Your life may feel like puzzle
pieces are scattered everywhere,
pieces here and way over there*

don't you dare show any fear

*God make no mistakes there is
nothing you can't bear*

breathe in the fresh air

*someday, one day, you'll see
those same pieces will come to
glee*

"Be the person who decided to go for it and didn't give up"

Be a go getter

Not a quitter

"Wear your crown with a

smile you deserve it Queen"

You are a Queen with a Dream

You deserve to be happy

to smile

to feel delightful

life is a blessing

so precious

so beautiful

take what you've been through

*turn it all around you'll feel much
better once lifted off the ground*

*walk with your head held high no
frown, smile my sister accessorize
with your beauteous crown*

"Be grateful and thankful for all things in life, never give up on YOU"

Begin this day with a smile on your face

a positive mind

and your day will be just fine

"*Dig deep down inside you*

will find that you can

weather any storm and

after the storm becomes a

beautiful rainbow"

There is sunshine after the storm

mixed with the rays of a beautiful rainbow

letting you know

you can't let go

it's not over until God says so

you never know

what your future may hold

no matter what, go and be bold

you will make it through hold on for a few, you could be closer to getting your breakthrough

the storm is just passing, you never know, just hold on, never let go -Never give up

Reminder. . .

No matter how many

curveballs, no matter how many setbacks,

No matter how much loss,

hurt or pain one must endure, the

person reading this book will

strive, survive, thrive and smile through it
all

I, Tomika Y. Reid encourage you to NEVER GIVE UP

through your storm(s)

be inspired by my quotes and poems

stand strong, rise up in a different form

you may appear to be weak

trust me, you got this

you are stronger than you think.

Inspire your way through

The Storm.